Habari's
BOOK OF
WORDS

The Basics of Reading for Early Learners

Lorraine Anderson and J. Cecil Anderson

This book features Red Dot•Best Spot™ Page Numbering—a numbering method that utilizes a red dot icon, to serve as a counting aid and guide for young readers when turning book pages. This extends reading enjoyment through proper book care and preservation.

RED DOT•BEST SPOT™
PAGE NUMBERING

Habari's Book of Words: The Basics of Reading for Early Learners • ISBN 979-8-218-69152-3

This book is to be used at the sole discretion and judgment of parents, caretakers and teachers.
Though not exhaustive, the content supports practices, processes and procedures of early childhood development.

Printed and manufactured in the United States of America

USING THIS BOOK

Reading is a vital building block of early childhood development. Reading sparks children's imagination and curiosity, and gives them a greater understanding of the world around them — and so much more. This book picks up where *Habari's Book of Letters: A Practical Guide for Learning the Alphabet* leaves off. Children will be introduced to word families, word recognition, rhyming, decoding, blending, high-frequency words, comprehension stories, sight words and word-building skills. The color-coded tabs are quick instructional guides, and promote engaged learning. As you work through the book, progress at a pace that is best for the child. **Have patience ... and have fun!**

The **Connect it!** tab helps children to associate an image with the target word. Have the child point to the image and name it.

The **Sound it!** tab directs children to sound out each letter of a word. Have the child point to each letter and vocalize it's sound.

The **Blend it!** tab directs children to blend letters together to hear the target word. Have the child vocalize each letter's sound, briefly holding (drag out) the sound of the second letter.

The **Read it!** tab directs children to read a word or a short, comprehension story. Have the child use their pointer finger to point to and read each word, slowly moving from left to right.

The **Share it!** tab directs children to share the story they read. After the child reads, allow them to express to you in their own words what each story is about. This helps build comprehension.

Let's Get More!
This part of the book offers added information for teaching and learning the basics of reading!

Did You Know?
In this part of the book Habari, our learning friend, highlights fun facts!

Let's Get Started!

WORD FAMILIES

Word families are groups of words that have a predictable pattern and rhythm — and they can rhyme! Learning word families provides critical skills necessary for reading.

-at | cat bat hat rat

10 **-en** | ten hen pen men

-ug | bug rug jug mug

Did You Know?

Exploring books, songs and poems is a wonderfully fun way to expose children to rhyming words. Also, they help develop "an ear" for the English language.

1

WORD FAMILIES

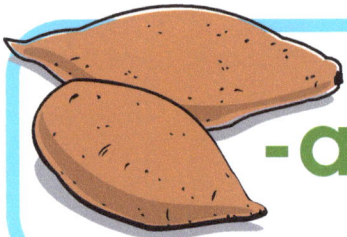

-am | yam jam ram dam

-an | can fan pan van

-un | sun fun run bun

-et | jet wet net pet

2

-at FAMILY

Connect it!

Sound it!

Blend it!

Read it!

/c/ /a/ /t/

/caaa/ /t/ cat

/b/ /a/ /t/

/baaa/ /t/ bat

3

-at FAMILY

/h / / a / / t /

/ haaa / / t / hat

/ r / / a / / t /

/ raaa / / t / rat

4

-en FAMILY

10

/t/ /e/ /n/

/teee/ /n/   ten

/h/ /e/ /n/

/heee/ /n/   hen

5

-en FAMILY

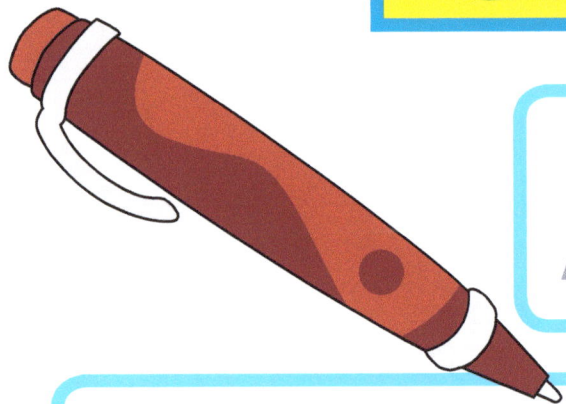

/p/ /e/ /n/

/peee/ /n/ pen

/m/ /e/ /n/

/meee/ /n/ men

6

-ug FAMILY

/b/ /u/ /g/

/buuu/ /g/ bug

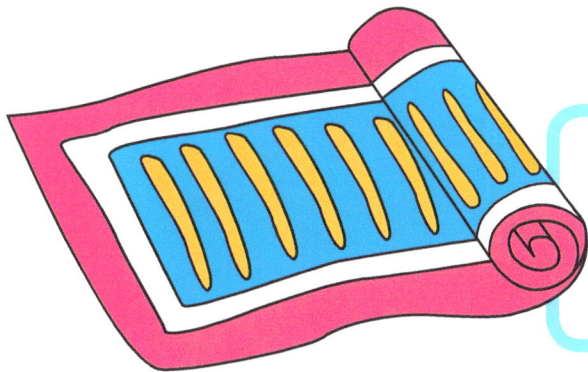

/r/ /u/ /g/

/ruuu/ /g/ rug

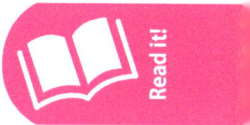

Connect it!
Sound it!
Blend it!
Read it!

7

-ug FAMILY

/j/ /u/ /g/

/juuu/ /g/ jug

/m/ /u/ /g/

/muuu/ /g/ mug

8

-am FAMILY

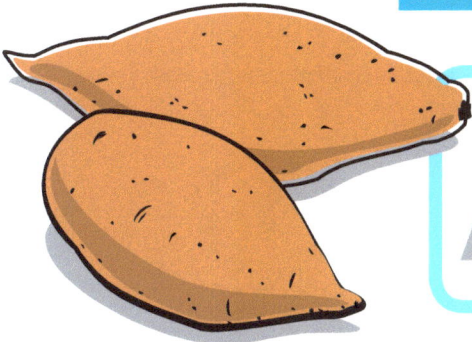

/ y / / a / / m /

/ yaaa / / m / yam

JAM

/ j / / a / / m /

/ jaaa / / m / jam

9

-am FAMILY

/r/ /a/ /m/

/raaa/ /m/ ram

/d/ /a/ /m/

/daaa/ /m/ dam

10

-an FAMILY

/c/ /a/ /n/

/caaa/ /n/   can

/f/ /a/ /n/

/faaa/ /n/   fan

-an FAMILY

/p/ /a/ /n/

/paaa//n/ pan

/v/ /a/ /n/

/vaaa//n/ van

12

-un FAMILY

/s/ /u/ /n/

/suuu/ /n/   sun

/f/ /u/ /n/

/fuuu/ /n/   fun

13

-un FAMILY

/r/ /u/ /n/

/ruuu/ /n/ run

/b/ /u/ /n/

/buuu/ /n/ bun

14

-et FAMILY

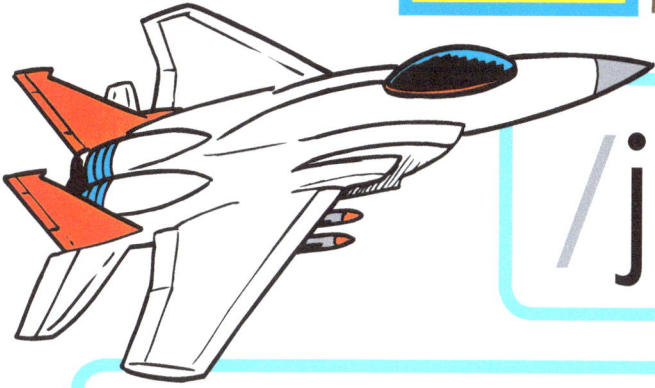

/j/ /e/ /t/

/jeee/ /t/ jet

/w/ /e/ /t/

/weee/ /t/ wet

15

-et FAMILY

/n/ /e/ /t/

/neee/ /t/ net

/p/ /e/ /t/

/peee/ /t/ pet

16

INTRODUCING HIGH-FREQUENCY WORDS

High-frequency words are those words that appear most frequently in written English. Early readers will soon hear and see these words readily in books that are read.

is	had	yes	if
in	a	it	and
at	has	I	his

Let's Get More!

THERE IT IS AGAIN!

Use fun games such as I Spy, Spell-N-Hop Hopscotch and Word Bingo to help children recognize high-frequency words.

Ben is ten.
Ben has a hen.
It is in a pen.

Pat and Mat sat in
a hat. Pat is a cat.
Mat is a rat.

Is it fun if I run
in the sun?
Yes, it is fun.

Sam is in a jet and
his pet. His pet sat
on a rug.

19

OTHER WORD FAMILIES

There are thirty-seven common word families in the English language. The next few pages will introduce several more word families to enhance the reading experience.

pin | win

fin | bin

20

mop] [top

hop] [pop

dad] [had

pad] [sad

21

map | cap

tap | nap

pot | not

hot | got

22

INTRODUCING SIGHT WORDS

Sight words are words that children learn to recognize by sight. With practice, they can read these words without sounding them out — helping with fluency in reading.

he	see	my
you	for	we
be	the	was
this	not	are
were	have	to

23

here	did	with
of	like	him
she	who	one
now	by	an
that	will	did
look		

Let's Get More!

YOUR OWN WORDS!

Use the Word Builders at the end of this book, to have the child build as many words as they can. Look for words from other books to build.

Meg **did** hop **to** get **my** mop.
It **was** at **the** top.

The pot **was** hot.
He got a pad **for** it.
Now it is not.

25

My dad had a map to look for his cap.
It was in the bin with a pin.
I was not with him.
I was with Tim.

Did you Know?

High-frequency words and sight words are often used interchangeably, but they do differ slightly. High-frequency words appear very often in text and can be sight words. Yet, sight words can be any words a reader has memorized and can easily recall when reading.

m	ap	og
p	en	ad
r	op	it
h	an	ut

t	ip	am
s	et	ot
d	ug	un
c	at	in

Let's Get a bit More!

BOOK LOVERS!

Celebrate reading at home by allowing children to see you read. Make time to read as a family. Take trips to your local library and check out books together — it's FREE!

Be sure to read aloud to children every night before bed. This builds a love for stories, books, reading, and it encourages oral communication.

WORD-WORTHY GAMES!

Earlier, we mentioned some games that build reading skills. **To play I SPY with words:** Start by writing high-frequency words or sight words on index cards. Add a different small sticker to the corner of each card. Lay the cards out on a flat surface. I SPY a sticker on a card and have the child say the word on that card.

this

To play Spell-N-Hop with words: Start by drawing a simple hopscotch grid with chalk. The grid can be made with sheets of paper taped together as well. Write high-frequency words or sight words in each space of the grid. Have children throw a small object onto the grid and then hop from word to word until they reach the object. The child will then spell the word in that space.

To play Word Bingo: The rules are basically the same as regular Bingo. The only difference is that high-frequency words or sight words are substituted for numbers. Ask family members to play for more fun.

MORE TO SHARE!

Get more information on preparing early learners for academic success via our **Getting the Brain Ready Virtual TalkShoppe** at: www.holychildpublications.com/talkshoppe

Holy Child PUBLICATIONS

ABOUT THE AUTHORS

Lorraine Anderson began her career as a teacher of technology for elementary students, teaching them to utilize computers for writing, reading, mathematics and art. She has taught in public school in California as well as in private and Title I schools in Georgia. In the capacity of support or lead, special needs, ESOL, communications liaison, kindergarten or pre-kindergarten teacher, Lorraine has been teaching and conferring with teachers to provide meaningful and individualized instruction for over 28 years.

She is passionate about literacy and helping students enjoy the overall experience of learning through incorporating projects and activities.

Additionally, she aspires to use her CELTA qualification to share her love for learning.

Lorraine enjoys reading, music, dance, live theater and outdoor activities.

J. Cecil Anderson has worked in Pre-K Education for over 14 years. He is passionate about literacy, teaching social skills and awakening student excitement for learning.

Cecil is a children's book author, illustrator, painter and graphic designer. He enjoys reading and outdoor activities and is an avid walker.